Practicing the Art of
COMPASSIONATE
LISTENING

Andrea S. Cohen

with Leah Green and
Susan Partnow

Practicing the Art of Compassionate Listening
February 2017, 2nd Edition

E-mail: cohencomm@gmail.com

ISBN 978-0-9830186-0-5

Book Cover by Linn DeNesti
Book design by Neva Welton
Graphics by Avril Orloff
Back Cover Photo by Johnny Bader

TABLE OF CONTENTS

FOREWORD

When we look into our own hearts and begin to discover what is confused and what is brilliant, what is bitter and what is sweet, it isn't just ourselves that we're discovering. We're discovering the universe.

– Pema Chodron

This book is a response to the many requests we've had over the years from participants in our programs who want to continue to practice the skills of Compassionate Listening, as well as those who have heard about our work and are looking for a way to experience it without coming to a training.

The book covers much of the material that we teach in our introductory trainings, including many of the exercises, and will help you understand and implement the practices of Compassionate Listening in your daily life. Whether you're challenged by your own self-judgments or by conflicts within your family, workplace or community, these practices can provide a solid foundation for bringing greater peace into your life, and to the world.

Our curriculum has evolved over many years of practice in conflict zones, as well as in hundreds of trainings right here at home. Our skilled facilitators work together as a learning community, sharing challenges and best practices with one another. We are truly an evolving community, and we consider each person who participates in our programs to be a contributing member.

We welcome you to the beginning of what we hope will be a lifelong journey, as it is for each one of us We are all senior trainers of this work, and have each experienced profound changes over the years since Compassionate Listening came into our lives. We've witnessed the changes in one another, and in our fellow facilitators and practitioners who have committed themselves to these practices. These internal shifts have given us confidence to bring Compassionate

Listening to wider and wider circles. And the success stories that participants from our trainings share with us inspire us to continue.

The skills you will learn may not be initially instinctive. But with continued practice, they will become more natural. It is somewhat like working out at a gym. At first, you must learn to do your practices correctly – and that takes good instruction, focus and effort. Then you begin to notice how good you feel, not only when working out but afterward as well. If you slack off for a while, though, you have to motivate yourself to get back into the habit. Sometimes, being coached by a skilled trainer can help you stay the course.

If you would like to understand the philosophy behind our work in greater depth, we recommend reading *Listening with the Heart: A Guide for Compassionate Listening,* by Carol Hwoschinsky, and *Compassionate Listening and Other Writings* by Gene Knudsen Hoffman, Edited by Anthony Manousos. To learn more about The Compassionate Listening Project and our workshops, delegations, books and videos – or to find a practice mentor – visit our website at www.compassionatelistening.org.

Whether you've participated in a Compassionate Listening program or this is your first exploration into the practices, we hope this book will be helpful to you.

In these difficult times, there is a great need for healing and connection. We offer this as a book of hope. Thank you for your interest in becoming a Compassionate Listener. It is a radical act that can help heal our world. Never doubt that we can make a difference – one person, one heart at a time.

Andrea Cohen, Leah Green and Susan Partnow

1. USING THE BOOK

Listening is a magnetic and strange thing, a creative force. The friends who listen to us are the ones we move toward. When we are listened to, it creates us, makes us unfold and expand.

- Karl Menninger

You stand to gain many skills by reading this book and doing the suggested exercises. Among them are:

- Listening to yourself and others with greater compassion.
- Avoiding the pitfalls of defensiveness and blame when disagreeing with others.
- Becoming attuned to the energy of conflict and intervening in a way that adds the wisdom of heart-to-heart listening to the equation.
- Creating a safe and respectful environment in which people can express their thoughts and feelings honestly.
- Doing your best to step into the shoes of another person to truly understand his or her perspective.
- Accessing your most authentic and solid self and encouraging the expression of another's deepest essence.

These are the foundational skills needed to transform the energy of conflict into an opportunity for connection, collaboration, and sustainable solutions. And they are skills we teach in our Compassionate Listening workshops. If you've taken a workshop, this book can help you remember what you did and guide you to additional practice. If you haven't yet taken a workshop, this introduction will help you reap some of the benefits of our work.

To deepen your understanding and experience of Compassionate Listening practice, we will invite you to do a number of exercises. Sometimes you will be able to do them on your own – in your mind's eye or simply with a pen and piece of paper. Other exercises require at least one other person. As our practices are meant to help you positively impact your relationship with yourself and others, it is important to try them with people in your life.

To get the full benefit of this work tackle just one chapter at a time, allowing yourself the opportunity for spacious reflection before immediately moving on to the next chapter. We talk about "slowing down to the speed of wisdom," and we invite you to give yourself that gift as you work through this book.

After each exercise, you might wish to journal about what you've experienced and would like to remember. We recommend designating a special notebook to use as your Compassionate Listening Practice Workbook and Journal.

SUPPORT FOR YOUR JOURNEY

Developing a structure to support you as you take this journey will be critical in helping you integrate these skills into your life. There are many ways to do that, and a combination of several of them may work best. For example:

- Keep a journal.
- Invite a friend to go through the book with you.
- Meet regularly with a group of friends or others in your community to try exercises together and talk about how the skills relate to challenging situations in your daily life. If you decide to do that, check out the Practice Group Manual you'll find on the Compassionate Listening website at www.compassionatelistening.org.
- Attend a Compassionate Listening Project workshop. These experiential workshops are a superb way to deepen your understanding and practice of the skills.

- Invite a certified Compassionate Listening Project facilitator to host a workshop in your area.

- Find a Compassionate Listening mentor to help you integrate the practices into real-life situations. (See "Meet Our Facilitators" on the Compassionate Listening website.) Although there are always obstacles along the way, life's challenges provide rich opportunities for learning. And the people with whom we are in conflict may be our greatest teachers.

Welcome to the Compassionate Listening journey!

Then we must listen. We must listen and listen and listen. We must listen for the Truth in our opponent, and we must acknowledge it. After we have listened long enough, openly enough, and with the desire to really hear, we may be given the opportunity to speak our truth. We may even have the opportunity to be heard. For no one and no one side is the sole repository of Truth. But each of us has a spark of it within. Perhaps, with compassion as our guide, that spark in each of us can become a glow, and then perhaps a light, and we will watch one another in awe as we become illuminated. And then, perhaps, this spark, this glow, this light will become the enlightening energy of love that will save all of us.

- Gene Knudsen Hoffman, "Speaking Truth to Power"

2. WHAT IS COMPASSIONATE LISTENING?

This listening requires a particular mode. The questions are non-adversarial. The listening is non-judgmental. The listener seeks the truth of the person questioned, and strives to see through any masks of hostility and fear to the sacredness of the individual, and discerns the wounds at the heart of any violence.

- Gene Knudsen Hoffman
Compassionate Listening pioneer

Compassionate Listening is a practice that integrates cognitive awareness with the wisdom of the heart. It fosters a quality of listening that helps create a safe setting for people to express themselves honestly and fully in search of their deepest truth.

Our practice is ultimately about healing our way to wholeness from the inside out. We believe that by opening and changing our hearts, we can contribute to changing the world – one person at a time. These are lofty ideals that require a commitment to the practices of Compassionate Listening skills without attaching to any particular outcome.

> *As some believe that "all politics are local," in Compassionate Listening we believe that in the context of human relationships "all peace is personal."*

The word compassion literally means *to suffer with*. To feel that depth of connection to another, we must find the place within us that also suffers. That requires the courage to look honestly and respectfully at our own internal landscape, filled with inconsistencies, conflict and difficult experiences – and the ability to hold it all with care. These are the same skills that we, as Compassionate Listeners, courageously offer to others.

We believe that within each individual is the essence of love and compassion. But as we move along our life journey, we suffer – whether from the pain of judgment, self-doubt, physical or mental abuse, or from the impacts of injustice, war, and poverty. Over the years, we have all developed layers of armor to protect ourselves. And that armor may manifest in one of many behaviors – perhaps as anger, blame, cynicism, physical attack, or withdrawal. Unfortunately, as we arm ourselves against others, we may also close ourselves off to the gifts of our deepest essence, allowing our hearts to shrivel and harden.

In the process of protecting ourselves, we also may commit the disservice of weaving together negative stories about ourselves or about the person who has harmed us. We may repeat the stories often and truly believe them. Sometimes these stories are about us as victims and the other person as victimizer, leaving little room for a different truth to emerge. Unfortunately, these negative stories can deplete our physical and mental energy and block access to one of our greatest assets – the wisdom of our hearts.

You might imagine the metaphor of *bricks and mortar* when thinking about this. The bricks refer to the specific incidents that caused us pain, often in our early years. And the mortar represents the stories we tell ourselves about these events that keep the bricks impermeable and locked in place. The structure we create can contribute to a physical sensation of feeling weighed down, isolated, and stuck. How often have you felt the burden of stuckness shrinking your heart, mind, and body?

Our work in Compassionate Listening is to re-open and strengthen the pathways back to our hearts, particularly when we're upset or in the heat of conflict. We seek to soften the mortar enough to allow our hearts to expand and enable a new perspective to emerge. This soft power requires us to become, in the words of Danaan Parry, true *warriors of the heart.*

OUR CORE PRACTICES

In Compassionate Listening, we teach a set of practices designed to help people access the wisdom of the heart for the sake of bringing greater peace and healing into their relationship with themselves and others. These practices are particularly useful in challenging situations where we tend to feel the most vulnerable and reactive – and often the least able to access our full wisdom and power. Accessing power for the highest good requires an integration of multiple sources of intelligence including head, heart, and body.

We believe the truest, deepest guidance lives within each one of us. It is not our job to fix others; rather, it is to help create the conditions that enable others to discover their own truth and trust their own wisdom to guide them through the murky waters of life's challenges.

Five Core Practices

- **Cultivating Compassion**- This includes developing empathy, experiencing and communicating gratitude, the ability to forgive, and the willingness to step into another person's shoes – seeing and feeling the world from their perspective to the extent that we can.

- **Developing the Fair Witness**- With this practice, we cultivate an ongoing process of self-exploration and the ability to hold both complexity and ambiguity. We learn to step out of a difficult interaction enough to notice what is happening on a meta level – in our minds, emotions, bodies, and spirit. We learn to recognize and contain our triggers and suspend judgment enough to stay connected and listen fully to another person's story and perspective. We learn to separate the impact of someone's words or actions from their intention.

- **Respecting Self and Others**- We take responsibility for our own part in what's unfolding and how we impact each other. We learn to hold healthy boundaries that are both protective and permeable, trusting that each of us has the capacity to resolve and heal our conflicts. Often just being heard allows us to take an important next step in that direction.

- **Listening with the Heart**- This skill requires quieting our minds so we can be fully present to others, genuinely seeking to know who they are, what they value, and the experiences that motivate their perspectives. Learning to listen with the heart, whether to ourselves or to another person, always opens doorways to deeper understanding. It requires shifting the focus from our active minds to the energetic core of our being, and keeping our own stories and interpretations out of the way. Then, listening with the heart is truly a gift.

- **Speaking from the Heart**- We seek to access and convey our own deep truth from as close to our own heart as we can get. The language we choose reflects a healing intention rather than words of blame or judgment that may trigger another's defenses. If we seek more information, it is out of genuine curiosity rather than to disprove the other person's point of view. We reframe issues to get at the essence of underlying needs and feelings. We courageously choose to give voice to what has truth and meaning – and do all of this for the sake of promoting healing.

Our Five Core Practices are easiest to access from the place of being centered and fully present, both to oneself and to another person. But what does that mean? A place of center is one where you feel anchored in the core of your being – in synchrony with the calm, clarity, and compassion that live there. When you are able to face your own internal landscape with this quality of being, you will provide a strong ballast for holding someone else's feelings and experiences – their pain, fears, and judgments – with equal care and respect.

Because the nature of the mind is to think, analyze, and evaluate, accessing the place of center can provide a great relief from this storm of internal activity. In this age of multi-tasking and over-stimulation, we all face the challenge of slowing down enough to access a state of calm and deeper awareness.

To the extent that we can tap into a solid, centered place, we will make better choices and healthier decisions. Perhaps the exponential ripple of these choices and decisions will help tip the balance toward greater peace and sustainability for our planet. Let's hope so!

CENTERING PRACTICES

In this book, we offer a number of activities that can help you find the place of *center*. Experiment with the meditative and self-reflective activities interspersed throughout the book and ask your friends for practices they use. Then, use the ones that work for you.

There are many types of practices to choose from. And you can do them in any environment – at home or in nature, alone or in a *sangha* (a word in Pali or Sanskrit that refers to a community with a common goal) at any time of day or night, or with any frequency that feels right to you.

Breath Meditation

A basic centering practice involves focusing on your breath. I recommend doing a breath meditation for 5-20 minutes on a regular basis. A simple daily practice, even if it's for just five minutes, can have a meaningful impact on your life.

Find a comfortable sitting position and allow yourself to become aware of your breath. Perhaps become aware of your chest and belly expanding and contracting as the breath flows freely and gently through your body...notice the air moving through your nostrils with each slow breath in... and out...

If you become aware of thoughts, just note them without judgment, let them go, and return to focusing on your breath... if feelings arise – perhaps of sadness or joy – allow them to surface and then let them go. If you become aware of sounds or bodily sensations, just notice them as well...let them go...and return to your breath. Be gentle with yourself...

This practice of noticing your thoughts, feelings and sensations will enhance the quality of your presence – with yourself and with others. You may want to use an image to help with the process of noticing and letting go. A friend imagines a tumbleweed propelled by a gentle breeze. The tumbleweed doesn't stick; it just lightly touches down and then floats away.

An additional benefit to having a regular centering practice is that it will help you return more quickly to a place of equanimity when you find a person or situation particularly troubling. This capacity is foundational to being a skilled Compassionate Listener able to maintain calm in the heat of conflict.

Quality Breathing

This exercise is something you can practice anywhere, any time, and as many times a day as you like. It's designed to help you focus on a positive quality you'd like to cultivate in your life – such as love, patience, compassion or gratitude – and breathe that intention in and through your heart. It may help to place your hand on your heart as you do this exercise. If you're not sure about which quality you'd like to integrate more fully into your being, try out a few and pay attention to your body's reaction as you do this. If at some point you find yourself smiling, or feeling some positive energy in your body, then this would be the quality to use – at least for now.

As you inhale slowly, imagine breathing that quality in through your nose, down your spine, through your heart, down through your belly – and then out. Do this slowly for a minute or two.

After this quality has become more integrated into your daily life, you may choose to focus on another quality using the same method.

Our very intention carries a great deal of power to shape what we believe and feel and, ultimately, how we show up in the world.

Grounding Meditation

The following meditation is adapted from the work of Margo Adair.

Find a comfortable sitting position. Let your inhale uplift your posture and your exhale soften your chest...Close your eyes and begin to focus on your breath...Move your attention to the area around the base of your spine...feel the energy there...sense a core of magnetic energy there...

As you exhale, imagine as though you were to drop a cord of energy from this center...down through the floor...all the way down...down into the earth...Imagine that this cord of energy sinks down through the soil...down, down into the ground... through the clay...through the underground waters...deeper and deeper through all the layers of the earth...each exhalation carrying it down further...until it settles in the center... like an anchor. Breathe out anything you want to release and transform...breathe it out and let gravity draw it down, absorbing any tensions...transforming it in the earth...

This energy cord can also bring earth energies up into your body...just like the trees draw nutrients into themselves...Feel the earth's energy coming up and moving through your whole body, grounding you in this present moment...

As the energy travels up and through you...feel yourself fully present...focused...relaxed...and supported...with all of the endurance, patience and courage you need...

When you are grounded, you are centered...

When you are ready, open your eyes, knowing that you can always find this place of center...and move through the day grounded, focused and clear...

Meditation on Self-Compassion

Our work is about healing the world from the inside out. It is critical to feel compassion for ourselves as we seek to take the gifts of Compassionate Listening into the world.

With eyes open or closed, bring to mind an image of yourself – perhaps even of you as a little baby or at another precious time…an image that evokes a sweet and gentle feeling within you. Breathe love and compassion through your heart into this image, whatever that may look and feel like. Imagine embracing yourself, holding yourself gently. You may want to touch your heart to help you anchor these feelings of tender self-compassion…

Now recall a special name for yourself, perhaps one a parent, partner or dear friend has called you. Speak this name to yourself…

Drink in these feelings of loving self-compassion.

Meditation on Expansive Compassion

After developing an abundance of self-compassion, you're ready to send it out to the world. This is an opportunity to explore how wide a circle of compassion you can create – starting with YOU. Dare to be expansive and take as much time as you need with this exercise.

With eyes open or closed, bring to mind an image of yourself that evokes a sweet and gentle feeling within you. Breathe love and compassion through your heart into this image. Then, slowly begin to expand your awareness to include those with whom you are closest – perhaps a child, a spouse, a friend, or even a pet. Anchoring in your heart, breathe love and compassion in and through this image of your loved ones.

Continue expanding the circle even further, spiraling out to the people in your neighborhood, your colleagues at work, and

*beyond...using whatever images speak to you. With each new
image, try to envision energy from your heart gently reaching from
you to the hearts of the other person or group you've brought to
mind. Allow this compassion spiral to reach as far as you can...
knowing that this is what our world needs for healing.*

People often ask whether even those who commit the most heinous
crimes are worthy of compassion. To the extent that we can recognize
a piece of ourselves in every other human being, the answer is an
unequivocal yes. As Alexander Solzhenitsyn said, "The line dividing
good and evil cuts through the heart of every human being."

You may find it easier to send compassion to people you feel are
the victims of injustice, rather than to the victimizers. Nonetheless, it
is important to remember that each person who causes suffering also
suffers. And that inside each of us lives the capacity for unskillful and
harm-causing behavior. The work of Compassionate Listening helps us
heal the divides within ourselves and bridge those that set us apart from
others. In the words of Compassionate Listening pioneer Gene Knudsen
Hoffman, "An enemy is someone whose story you haven't yet heard."

JOURNALING

Journaling is a wonderful self-reflective activity that can give you
insight into your current thoughts, feelings and bodily sensations. It
brings you into the present moment to explore fully what's alive for
you. If you choose to journal, let your thoughts flow freely – no need
to judge or edit them in any way. Journaling should be for you and
you alone, perhaps an all-too-rare opportunity to listen to yourself
without trying to fix, mask, or push away what's there. Remember to
hold yourself with compassion as you allow things to surface.

Some people prefer to journal with pen and paper, while others
prefer to use their computer. What I find particularly useful is to
close my eyes while writing at the computer. That allows me to plumb
the depths of my thoughts and feelings without the interruption of
more mundane concerns, such as wanting to ensure that my spelling
and grammar are correct. It's simply a quick and easy method of
expression – solely for me.

I might journal about the same situation again within a day or two, or even the following week. It's interesting to see my perspective shift, literally before my eyes, just because I've allowed myself freely, and without judgment, to express my truth.

Journaling on Compassion

The intent of this journaling exercise is to explore the issue of compassion in your life. Make this reflection as deep and honest an experience as you can.

Identify a personal situation or relationship that currently brings you anger, pain, sadness or despair and write about it from your heart – without judgment, analysis or a plan for resolution or fixing. Reflect on the following:

- What personal situation or relationship currently brings you anger, sadness, or despair? If there is more than one, choose the one you'd most like to explore.
- Who are you least able to feel compassion for in this situation?
- Who are you most able to feel compassion for in this situation?
- What's your vision of the way you'd like this relationship to be?
- What else would you like to understand?

Give yourself the time to explore each question fully. At the end of your journaling session, give yourself compassion for your suffering and appreciation for your courage to explore its deeper meaning.

TAKE-AWAY SUGGESTIONS

When you find yourself reacting with anger, fear, sadness, or despair to a conflict and its painful ramifications, take a moment to notice what is happening for you. Do a centering practice before taking any other action. Then engage in self-inquiry: What are you feeling? What are you most wanting? What values do you hold that are longing to be respected? Give yourself the space to slow down to the speed of wisdom. Center yourself and reflect on the situation, without attachment to a particular outcome. This is an important first step toward deeper understanding and healing.

Additional Resources

Adair, Margo. *Working Inside Out*. Sourcebooks MediaFusion, 2003.

Hwoschinsky, Carol. *Listening With the Heart*, 4th edition, Indianola, WA. The Compassionate Listening Project, 2006.

Palmer, Wendy. *The Intuitive Body: Discovering the Wisdom of Conscious Embodiment and Aikido*. North Atlantic Books, 2008.

Parry, Danaan. *Warriors of the Heart*. BookSurge Publishing, 2009.

3. LISTENING BASICS

Listening has the quality of the wizard's alchemy. It has the power to melt armor and to produce beauty in the midst of hatred.

– Brian Muldoon

While hearing is something humans do naturally due to our biology, good listening is a far more skillful process. Most of us have experienced the frustration of not feeling fully listened to – without the interference of another's judgment, personal story, or interruption. And we have all witnessed that when people talk about hot topics, good listening skills can totally evaporate. Often, the attempted dialogue devolves into heated debate and hardened polarization of perspectives.

How many of us have listened long enough to find the flaw in another person's thinking, gathering all the arguments we can muster to make them *wrong* and us *right*? Or have our minds go off on their own tangent after something triggers a memory or personal story? When we interject our own reaction, story, or even questioning into the situation, we risk changing the course of what might have emerged had we been able to take our hands off the steering wheel and simply listen.

ANOTHER WAY TO LISTEN

There is another way to listen, and that's what these next few exercises are about. You will need to do them with at least one other person. Find a friend, relative, colleague, or community member to practice with before you begin. After you have found someone to practice with, begin the next sequence of exercises. Spend time to debrief with your partner after each exercise.

Being Present

The quality of your presence impacts others. How comfortable are you when you're face to face with another person? Do you look at people when you speak – or do you find it difficult to maintain eye contact? Are you distracted with thoughts or judgments? Are you comfortable with silence? Do you tend to fill empty spaces with the sound of your own voice?

This exercise provides an opportunity for you to explore what happens when you're in the presence of another person...in silence. Allow yourself three to five minutes for the exercise.

Facing your practice partner, you'll begin with your eyes closed. Spend a few minutes just being with yourself with gentleness and compassion. When you've found a place of equanimity, continue by opening or closing your eyes at will. During the exercise, your eyes may be open or closed at any given moment – and your partner's eyes can be either open or closed as well. You may be looking at each other at some point – or not. If you lose your equanimity, do whatever you need to do to re-ground and return to your center.

There is no right way to be or to feel. The point of the exercise is simply for you to notice your reactions: your feelings, your thoughts, the sensations in your body, the judgments you are making about yourself or the other person – or even your judgments about the exercise itself. Continue to notice as your thoughts or feelings change. After finishing this exercise, talk to your partner or journal about what you experienced.

Listening without Speaking

Good listening is a gift of great proportion. It nourishes both parties by providing the time and space to speak and be listened to without another person's agenda steering the course. And what it requires is something simple – the intention to be and remain fully present.

In this exercise, you will take turns being in the role of Speaker and Listener. Each person will have an equal amount of time (three to five minutes) to speak without interruption about what arises when reflecting on the suggested theme. It's a good idea to use a timer to ensure that each person has the same amount of uninterrupted time to be heard. Staying in integrity with the following set-up guidelines will help you get the most out of this exercise.

Listener:

- Be fully present for your partner without the use of words.
- Direct your energy to the area of your heart as you listen to your partner.
- Allow yourself to feel nourished by this process.
- Don't interrupt or interject comments (this is very important).
- When you find your mind wandering, bring yourself back to keeping your heart open and just listening without judgment or analysis.

Speaker:

- Take a moment to reflect on the sentence *"One place where I'm currently feeling challenged in my life is…"*
- Focus your breath on the area around your heart before beginning to speak.
- Speak from your heart without judging or analyzing your words.
- Silence is OK.
- This time is for you, rather than for entertaining your listener.
- Allow yourself to take a risk and be vulnerable.
- Slow down to notice if you're staying connected with your heart as you speak; re-focus your energy there, if it's needed.

Step-By-Step Guidelines:

1. Decide who will begin as Speaker and who will begin as Listener, allotting an equal amount of time for each person's turn. Then begin.

2. When the time is up, take a moment to reflect silently on what you've heard yourself say, as speaker – and as listener, to what your partner has shared.

3. Switch roles, with both people returning to a heart-centered focus.

4. When finished, again, self-reflect (step 2 above).

5. Thank your partner for the quality of listening you received.

Journaling:

Participants in our workshops are often surprised at what arises when another person listens deeply, with a loving presence that allows a speaker to go in whatever direction is needed. Take a moment to write in your journal about the exercise. You may want to share some of what you experienced with your partner.. Here are some things you might want to address:

When you were speaking...

- What did the listener do that made you feel s/he was truly present?

- How was this different than the way you're normally listened to?

- What did you appreciate?

- Anything else...

When you were listening...

- How was this different from the way you normally listen?

- What did you appreciate in this process?

- What were you aware of that felt uncomfortable?
- Was there anything that made you feel relieved about being in this role?
- Anything else…

What would you like to remember about this exercise? Is there someone in your life you'd like to listen to in this way?

REFLECTIVE LISTENING

Listening with your heart to another person is a great honor. And being listened to without judgment or interruption by a person who is centered in the heart is an all-too-rare gift.

Reflective listening takes the listener one step further in being able to be of service to another person. When people hear the details of what's important to them reflected back, a whole new world of awareness and understanding opens up.

Why is reflective listening so important in Compassionate Listening practice? It helps deepen our understanding of another's experience and ensures that we're hearing accurately what the other person is saying. So often, we read into another person's story our own meaning and interpretation without even realizing it, which can easily result in misunderstanding and miscommunication. Even more importantly, when someone hears reflections that strike a deep internal chord, greater clarity and understanding often emerge spontaneously.

Listening for Facts, Feelings and Values

This is one of the most important exercises in Compassionate Listening. You'll learn to listen with your ears, eyes, and heart to multiple layers of a person's story, reflect back what you think you've heard and check for accuracy. It is about getting as close to the heart of what matters to the speaker as you can, without asking questions.

Facts- The facts are about what actually happened – what you could see or hear if you viewed a videotape of the situation. Many people find this layer of information easy to listen for, although for others it is a great challenge. Listen for the 'headlines' rather than for every detail in the story, or notice what facts had the strongest impact on you.

Feelings- Listening for the feelings, whether revealed explicitly or implicitly, adds another layer of information to the Compassionate Listening intention. Among the feelings you may pick up in the speaker's telling of a story may be sadness, frustration, happiness, pride, fear, anger, or something else. In fact, through the course of relating a single story a person is likely to cycle through many different feelings. Pay close attention to the speaker's facial expressions and body language, which are often a window into the deeper feelings at play.

Values- The values embedded in a story provide us with yet a third layer of richness, and these refer to what a person holds to be important at the core of his or her being. Does the speaker value family? Trust? Respect? Truth? Connection? Compassion? Something else? These are the jewels that explain why the speaker has chosen to tell you this story and what its deepest meaning might be…to the speaker.

Rather, it is about simply noticing and reflecting back the layers of information offered within a single story and checking to make sure that what you've picked up is accurate. It is about getting as close to the heart of what matters to the speaker as you can.

Step-By-Step Guidelines for Dyads:

In this exercise, you will be listening to another person – perhaps a family member, friend or colleague. The two roles are Speaker and Listener.

Speaker:

1. Think about something that has happened recently that is still moderately upsetting to you. Choose a personal situation that you'd like more insight into.

2. Take about three minutes to share your story with the listener. It's important to remember to be brief and to the

point in telling your story. The listener doesn't need to know all of the background. Getting lost in the story, particularly if it's a story you've repeated many times, can deepen the grooves with which this story gets stuck in place.

Listener:

1. Center yourself and listen as fully as you can to the three layers of the story.

2. Work to set aside judgments, interpretations or reactions.

3. When the speaker is through sharing the story, begin your process of reflection. First, reflect back the major facts that you heard. After each reflection, ask the speaker if what you heard was accurate, and allow time for the speaker to respond. When you're done, ask the speaker if you left out anything important.

4. Reflect back the feelings you heard expressed or saw or intuited with your heart. When possible, link the feelings you reflect with the part of the story they go with. After each feeling that you reflect, check for accuracy and give the speaker an opportunity to clarify. Be spacious – it will likely take longer for the speaker to get in touch with his/her feelings than it took for the facts. Before moving on, ask the speaker if you missed anything.

5. Finally, reflect back the speaker's deeply held values you picked up from the story. Just name them, without explaining your reasoning – and ask if this rings true to your speaker. Again, allow the speaker time to respond and clarify.

It's important to be deeply respectful in the reflection process. Always ask the speaker if what you think you heard is accurate. Avoid analysis, interpretation, and offering advice. Projecting your meaning onto your speaker's story is a great disservice to the unique individual to whom you're listening.

Simple reflection provides a wonderful opportunity for discernment. For example, when reflecting back "I thought you were feeling angry when your boss reminded you that you hadn't done something you'd agreed to do," the speaker might say, "No, I wasn't angry. I realize I was scared."

Reflecting back what you think you've heard offers an opportunity for the speaker to refine his/her understanding of why this situation is disturbing. Often, solutions or next steps naturally emerge from this process.

If focusing on all three layers of the story at one time is too difficult, focus your listening on values. That's because many of us are unaccustomed to focusing on values when we listen to another's story, and it's often an extremely important layer for the listener to hear when it's reflected back.

After you've completed this, switch roles and repeat the process.

Journaling

Take a moment to reflect and write in your journal. Here are some things you might think about:

- As a speaker, which type of reflection was most meaningful to you?

- Did you learn something you didn't know before? If so, what was it?

- In what ways, if any, did your relationship to this situation shift?

- As a listener, which level of the story – facts, feelings or values – was easiest for you to listen for? Which information was most difficult for you to listen for?

- What would you like to remember about this exercise?

Listening for Facts, Feelings and Values- Variations

Once you've practiced in dyads, try Listening for Facts, Feelings and Values using any of the following variations.

Small Groups:

If you're doing this exercise in small groups, each listener will concentrate on only one part of the story – either facts, feelings or values. If you have one or more groups of 4, each person can rotate through and experience every role: speaker, listener for facts, listener for feelings and listener for values. If you have uneven numbers, add a listener for body language. (See "Variation: Listening for Body Language" below.)

Large Groups:

1. Sitting in a circle, invite a speaker to come to the front to share a story.

2. Before the speaker begins, break the group into 3 sections: listeners for facts, listeners for feelings and listeners for values, and go over the instructions for the speaker and the listeners.

3. After the story, those in the *Facts* section are invited to offer their reflections, carefully following guidelines for listeners above.

4. Move next to the *Feelings* section and finally to the *Values* section.

5. Offer appreciation to the speaker as a very short closing round.

Listening for Body Language:

Add another listener to listen to the speaker's body language. Paying close attention to a person's facial expressions and body gestures as s/he tells the story is often very revealing. You might notice nuances in posture, excitement level or facial expressions at various points in the story's telling. A sigh of relief or clenched fist can say a great deal about a speaker's relationship to different parts of his or story. In our workshops, people often find this level of information to be surprising, enlightening and even amusing.

Example of Facts, Feelings and Values

Barbara (Speaker): *Last week I had a very upsetting conversation with my sister Carol. I called her to see how she was and she told me that her husband Carl lost his job. Of course, she was very upset about it. She went on and on about the owners of the company being Asian – and launched into a tirade about immigration, saying that's what happens when you let too many foreigners immigrate. Not only do they take jobs from Americans, but they also end up costing us in other ways by getting services that real Americans should be getting.*

Carol and I are different politically, and I know she was upset because Carl lost his job. But for her to generalize to all Asians, let alone all immigrants, seemed so unfair – and it actually made me angry. My father-in-law, whom I love dearly, emigrated from Japan a long time ago/. I just felt really bad that my own sister would be so prejudiced – and I don't want to have to choose between loyalties.

What are some facts that a listener can reflect?

- Barbara called her sister Carol to find out how she was.
- Barbara found out Carol's husband had lost his job.
- The company Carol's husband worked for is owned by Asians.

- Carol said this country lets too many foreigners immigrate.

What are some feelings you picked up when the person was speaking? Examples might be:

- Sadness
- Anger
- Hurt
- Frustration
- Disappointment

What values might be embedded in Barbara's telling of her story? Examples might be:

- Family
- Compassion
- Fairness
- Loyalty
- Justice

What body language did you notice?

In Barbara's story, perhaps she was hunched over, looking down, and averting eye contact with the listener(s) in the beginning. But, when she talked about Carol generalizing about all Asians, perhaps she was looking up fiercely and her fists were clenched. When reflecting back, those pieces of information may be useful to Barbara.

TAKE-AWAY SUGGESTIONS

1. As you did in the *Listening without Speaking* exercise, think about someone in your life you'd like to just listen to in silence and with full presence. When the time is right, try doing this for even five minutes and see what emerges. Become aware of your natural inclination – which might be to interrupt, fix, or tell your own story. If your mind wanders or you're snagged into judgment, upset, or disagreement, note that reaction and return to being fully present for the other person. It might help to imagine being literally connected – perhaps by an imaginary umbilical cord – from your heart to theirs. Give them the gift of full presence that we all long for!

2. When entering a listening opportunity that could prove challenging, you might want to begin by bringing to awareness at least one thing you truly appreciate about the other person. It could be a quality, value or commitment you respect. One example might be the value of family, fairness, or a strong work ethic. Look for anything that helps you open your heart, even if the two of you are in conflict.

3. Begin listening to someone with the intention of identifying layers of the story to reflect back. No one need know that you're practicing Compassionate Listening as you do this. But it is likely to have a qualitative impact on your own experience – as well as on that of the other person. This is particularly true if you are listening and reflecting from your heart, rather than simply doing the activity as a mechanical exercise. There may be people or situations where reflecting back and naming someone's feelings may not be welcomed. Use your discretion, and avoid the arrogance of telling someone what they're feeling rather than suggesting that this is what you thought you picked up.

4. If you find your attention drifting when someone is talking about a situation that s/he is concerned or upset about, focusing on any level of the person's story (facts, feelings, values or body language) will bring you back into being more fully present.

5. If someone gives you the gift of listening deeply, thank them. Remembering to offer gratitude is a wonderful heart-opening opportunity for us as well as for the other person. Developing the habits of both offering it and allowing it to "land" when offered to us helps strengthen our compassion capacity for the sake of all who need it - which means…all of us.

4. THE HEART MATTERS

To develop the drop of compassion in our own heart is the only effective spiritual response to hatred and violence.

— Thich Nhat Hanh

Much has been written about how interconnected the activity in our own brain is with the brain of another – and how what we see impacts what we feel and what we do. Dr. Daniel Siegel, author of *The Mindful Brain,* writes about how our brains are wired to mirror the feelings in another's brain. We are literally wired to feel compassion when we connect with the suffering of another person or when we witness a compassionate act.

Through research in the relatively new field of neurocardiology, we also know that the state of our hearts has a powerful impact on our own bodies as well as on others in our environment. Neuroscientists are providing the proof to ground what people have sensed intuitively for a very long time.

Scientists used to view the heart as simply a pump that delivers blood to different parts of the body. However, researchers now recognize that, with its own brain center and neural cells, the heart is a sophisticated mechanism for receiving and processing information. In addition to this extensive neural communication network linking the heart with the brain and the rest of the body, the heart also generates the body's most powerful electromagnetic field.

Using equipment such as magnetic resonance imaging devices (MRIs) and electrocardiograms (ECGs), scientists are now able to measure the positive impact of the heart on our physical, emotional and mental states.

THE HEART IS POWERFUL

The heart contains approximately 40,000 neural cells – the kind we used to think existed only in the brain. It's estimated that 60-65% of the heart's cells are neural cells. In fact, the heart sends many more messages to the brain than the brain sends to the heart. And through a process called Entrainment, our brain's rhythms naturally synchronize to our heart's rhythms, rather than the other way around.

In the world of the physical sciences, entrainment, a law of physics discovered by the Dutch scientist Christian Huygens in 1665, has been well recognized for a long time. For example, if a tuning fork that's designed to produce a frequency of 440 Hz is struck (causing it to oscillate) and is then brought into the vicinity of another 440 Hz tuning fork, the second tuning fork will begin to oscillate as well. The first tuning fork is said to have entrained the second tuning fork.

Other examples of entrainment in the physical world include:

- If you have a room full of pendulum-type grandfather clocks and start the pendulums in motion at different times, they will all swing differently. However, if you walk out of the room and return a few days later, all of the pendulum movement cycles will have come into synchrony.
- The blinking frequency of fireflies can be influenced by others of the same species. When thousands of fireflies gather in one location, their blinking frequency becomes synchronized – and in just a few seconds all of the blinking becomes entrained.

In the human environment, a similar phenomenon occurs. Often without noticing what's happened, we begin to resonate with each other's emotional states. A negative consequence of this phenomenon occurs when we witness mob behavior as it's caught by others – almost like a virulent virus. On the positive side, the converse is also true. For example, a person in an agitated state can often be calmed down by the presence of someone who is in a palpable state of equanimity.

The power of our intention is critical. When we experience feelings of appreciation, love, or compassion, our heart rhythms shift and direct new electromagnetic impulses to our brain. Just by holding a compassionate emotional state we can counteract our own judgment, anxiety, resentment, and hatred. Positive behavior toward another person is more likely to result from this state than from one where we have strong negative judgments about the other person.

The heart impacts our body's well-being. The state of our heart affects our other bodily organs, their chemical and hormonal output, and our immune system. When we're anchored with compassionate and altruistic thoughts, our bodies achieve their highest physiological state of health.

A Harvard study divided subjects into two groups. One group watched an emotionally neutral movie and the other group observed Mother Teresa helping poor people in Calcutta. Those who saw Mother Teresa's altruism on-screen turned out to have "markedly higher levels" of immunoglobulin A in their saliva. The Harvard researchers coined the term "Mother Teresa effect" to describe how merely watching an act of altruism can be good for you.

Scientists comparing meditation practices that focus on the breath or emptying the mind with meditation practices that focus on compassion, joy, or gratitude have found that the latter have a markedly better impact on the body's immune system. Taken a step further, perhaps we can infer that practicing acts of compassion can help heal us, both as individuals and as a society.

THE HEART'S ENERGY FIELD IS CONTAGIOUS

The heart's electromagnetic field is several thousand times more powerful than the brain's electromagnetic field, and it expands at least six to eight feet beyond our body. When we shift our own physiology, we literally shift the physiology and brain waves of others in our sphere.

One study found that Tibetan Buddhist monks who practice holding compassionate thoughts on a daily basis radiate a stronger electromagnetic field than monks who simply practice holding relaxed meditative states.

Those of us who conduct listening sessions in conflict and post-conflict zones feel the power of the energetic field we create. A physical space filled with loving and compassionate people creates an extremely safe container for holding the pain of personal stories our witnesses share. This is a healing experience for both speakers and listeners, with a potential ripple effect beyond measure.

The heart is the seat and lifeblood of our collective humanity. States of heart that reflect love, compassion, joy, and appreciation literally help us to thrive – as individuals and as a species. What science is confirming is that our state of being has a profound impact on the world around us.

> *For me it was the crucial experience of the last years to encounter Jewish people who met me, the child of Nazi Germans, without hatred, with peaceful hearts, simply as a human being. I would never have dared to hope for that! This experience brought about for me that I could release a huge part of the burden of guilt that I had taken over from my parents unconsciously. This was a great relief for me. Thanks for helping me with it!*
>
> *-Participant, German–Jewish Reconciliation project*

PRACTICAL IMPLICATIONS

The emotional states we cultivate impact us, as well as the people around us. When we are able to feel our own and another's suffering, we are more likely to see ourselves *in* the other. Holding compassion for the other increases the likelihood of positive actions that promote the alleviation of suffering rather than the causing of it.

The converse is also true. If we cultivate anger, judgment, and blame toward others, our thoughts become more polarizing (*us* versus *them*) and our actions more oppositional. When we identify others as "the problem" or "evil" or "the enemy," it is easier to justify an action designed to harm them. We fail to see the deeper positive essence that dwells within them – and the threads of commonality that all humans share, such as the need for safety, belonging, and respect, as well as the capacity for goodness.

The challenge then is: *How do we use the power of our hearts to bring greater peace to our world – to ourselves, our families, our workplaces and our communities?*

LISTENING AND SPEAKING FROM THE HEART

The heart needs regular attention to help it perform for the highest good. We cultivate compassion simply by focusing our attention on our hearts. Then we can begin to practice what it feels like to listen and speak from our heart's center.

Listening with and speaking from the heart are acts of both intention and attention. First, you must want to do it; and second, you must be able to move energy from a more cerebral place to the area around your heart. If you're listening and speaking from the head, you're more likely to do so with judgment and analysis – a narrowing of focus. Listening with and speaking from the heart, on the other hand, are acts of openness, generosity and compassion.

When speaking, it is not only about what you say, but it's also about where you say it from in your body and what your intention is in saying it. Sometimes we hear people's words, but don't believe their authenticity. When the words are grounded in a felt sense, people's hearts open.

When your heartfelt truth reaches another person's heart, the resulting connection is likely to be a positive one – even if what you're expressing is difficult for the person to hear. The language you use when speaking from your heart will lack the blame and judgment that create polarity and separation.

Listening with and speaking from the heart are acts of courage. (In fact, the word *courage* comes from *coeur* – which, in French, means *heart*.) It takes courage to speak about your personal experiences, feelings, and even your fears. And it takes courage to listen so openly to someone else's experience that the possibility exists for you to be changed by what you hear.

What follows are two scenarios that take place in Israel and Palestine – one that leads to separation, and one that leads to heart-to-heart connection.

Hisham is 32 years old. He lives in the West Bank and has been imprisoned by the Israeli military numerous times, as have most of his friends. He has never known a Palestine without occupation, and longs for the time when he can travel with a Palestinian passport. Joe, a Jewish American, travels to Hisham's town to visit biblical sites. By chance, they meet at a café and begin talking.

Scenario 1

Joe: *What a great place – old tombs of sages. So much incredible history.*

Hisham: *Well you're a tourist, just try living here! Where are you from, the U.S.?*

Joe: *Yeah... so?*

Hisham: *This is a prison. The Israelis treat us like we're nobody – worse than nobody. Trash. Meanwhile they live like kings and we live under constant threat of violence and oppression. And the U.S. just keeps on giving them money. Everyone here hates your country. You're all alike – wanting to see our antiquities here, but you don't care about the Palestinians who live here. You don't have a clue what it's like to live here.*

Joe: *C'mon. That's not the whole story and you know it! What about your side? What about Palestinian violence? (a debate ensues)*

Scenario 2

Joe: *What a great place – old tombs of sages. So much incredible history.*

Hisham: *Well you're a tourist, just try living here! Where are you from, the U.S.?*

Joe: *Yeah… so?*

Hisham: *This is a prison. The Israelis treat us like we're nobody – worse than nobody. Trash. Meanwhile they live like kings and we live under constant threat of violence and oppression. And the U.S. just keeps on giving them money. Everyone here hates your country. You're all alike – wanting to see our antiquities here, but you don't care about the Palestinians who live here. You don't have a clue what it's like to live here.*

Joe: *(silence and with deep concern) I'm sorry things are so hard. Would you be willing to tell me more about what your day-to-day life is like? I've never had the chance to meet a Palestinian before.*

Hisham: *It's really tough living under occupation. We can't go anywhere - we're locked in by endless Israeli checkpoints. I can't travel or find work, and without work I can't marry, so I have no future. There are no human rights – every man I know has been in and out of prison and we never know what the charge is. Our land has been taken for settlements. We've lost any hope for our own state. It seems like the whole world has forgotten us…. (silence)*

Joe: *(silence)*

The first time around, Joe and Hisham quickly polarize and their conversation deteriorates into fierce debate, which is ultimately a lose/lose situation.

In the second scenario, Joe reflects back the sense of difficulty he picks up from Hisham and asks him to say more about it. Trusting that Joe is really interested and perhaps even cares, Hisham begins to speak from his heart about his own experience. He doesn't label, blame, or judge. The result? Joe and Hisham continue to dialogue. Nothing is solved in that moment, but a door to understanding and deeper connection is opened.

ACCESSING THE POWER OF YOUR HEART

The best way to access the power of your heart is through doing some type of heart-centered breathing on a regular basis. The more you practice this, the easier it will be to move the energy to that part of your body in difficult situations – when you're upset or deeply triggered by someone else's position or by your own painful past experiences. We deal more with the issue of triggers in Chapter 6.

Committing to Compassionate Listening practice requires the same dedication as committing to a regular program of physical fitness. You work to strengthen your muscles for months. But it's only when you attempt to move something really heavy or walk a marathon that you realize your muscles are strong enough to carry the load.

The following meditations can help keep the heart muscles working optimally for the sake of bringing peace and healing to us, our families, workplaces, communities, and beyond. To experience them fully, you may want to record these meditations (or make up your own) and play them back when you're ready to practice.

Heart-Focus Meditation

You can do the following meditation while sitting, standing or lying down in a comfortable position you can maintain for 10-15 minutes. It's a wonderful way to begin or end your day.

Slowly bring your attention to your breath as it flows in and out. As you inhale, allow the air gently to push your belly out. As you exhale, consciously relax your belly so that it feels soft. Practice this focusing of your attention for an extended time.

Now breathe to the area of your heart...Draw attention to your heart... Smile to your heart... Recall to yourself your name of endearment as a beloved... Bring to mind either a memory of an experience with another person when you had a powerful feeling of loving or being loved... or a scene in nature that fills you with joy and tranquility.

When the image of that experience is clear in your mind, try to re-experience in the present moment the associated peaceful and loving feelings. Imagine these good feelings are centered deeply in your heart...

Hold those peaceful feelings for as long as you can. If you find that your attention wanders, return to your breath and the unforced rise and fall of your stomach...Then come back to your heart... Smile to your heart. Spend some time in this gentle place of nourishing your heart.

When you are ready, slowly open your eyes...and imagine bringing this sweet energy with you throughout your day.

Widening Your Circle of Compassion

As we did in Chapter 2, experiment with how wide a circle of compassion you can create. Dare to be expansive and reach beyond your comfort zone.

As you do this meditation on compassion imagine yourself sitting in a setting you love – perhaps in a beautiful, open field, on a sandy beach, or next to a mountain stream.

Close your eyes and allow yourself to feel your connection to the earth and the beauty in your midst. Allow the calm to permeate your being...to move through every cell in your body...

Let go of thoughts, feelings, and sensations...Observe your breath flowing in and out...easily and freely. See the sun spreading its golden glow above your head...illuminating the horizon without end. Imagine its warm glow streaming through you, breathing life, warmth and calm into your heart...

Now imagine someone you deeply love – perhaps a child, a parent, a spouse or trusted friend – or even a pet. See the warm, golden light of love streaming to and flowing through this being. See this beloved being surrounded by the light of love and kindness and happiness.

Now, bring to mind a person with whom you have a neutral relationship – perhaps someone with whom you have a more distant connection. And see the warm, golden light of love streaming to and flowing through this being. See this person surrounded by the light of love and kindness and happiness...

Finally, think of someone you have difficulty with or maybe someone you actively fear or dislike. Imagine the warm, golden light of love streaming to and flowing through this being. If this is difficult, try seeing this person, perhaps as a very young child, surrounded by the light of love and kindness and happiness...

Imagine all of these people together with you, with the sun above –receiving the warm golden light of loving-kindness. Then let them go in peace and happiness...

Slowly, return to yourself and focus on breathing deeply and slowly. See that same golden light surrounding you with love and gentleness... When you're ready, open your eyes...

Loving-Kindness (Metta) Meditation

This is a loving-kindness meditation based in the Buddhist tradition. It is a nice way to complete any other meditation – either silently or by speaking it out loud.

May I be free from pain...may I be free from suffering...may I be healed...may I live in peace

May you be free from pain...may you be free from suffering... may you be healed...may you live in peace

May we be free from pain...may we be free from suffering... may we be healed...may we live in peace

May all beings be free from pain...may all beings be free from suffering...may all beings be healed...and may all beings live in peace.

Gratitude and Appreciation Practice

Taking the time to bring gratitude and appreciation into conscious awareness helps us to integrate the practice of Cultivating Compassion into our daily lives. As with our other practices, doing this may not initially feel comfortable. However, in time you're likely to welcome its rightful place in the fabric of your life.

Options for practice that take only a minute or two:

- *Gratitude for the other.* When you're with people you care about, take a moment verbally to express your appreciation for them – from your heart.

- *Appreciation for yourself.* Use the following opening to recount some things you truly value about yourself: "What I appreciate about myself is..." When you do this, connect with the goodness that dwells at the core of your being and speak the words with conviction.

Self-appreciation is a particularly wonderful practice that can help counteract the voices of negative self-judgment that accompany so many of us as we move through our daily activities. For many people, true self-appreciation without qualification is one of the most difficult things they do in Compassionate Listening practice. For that reason alone, try it!

And, when people express appreciation for *you*, allow it in with as much fullness, grace, and ease as you can. Watch for any temptation on your part to minimize or dismiss this gift. For example, if you catch yourself responding something like "oh, I didn't really do anything..." – stop – and just let the words of gratitude or appreciation sink in.

TAKE-AWAY SUGGESTIONS

1. Repeat any of these meditations as many times as you like and in any situation – even when you feel anger, fear, hatred, or other difficult emotions. This requires a willingness to shift your attention from the difficult feelings and allow the energy of pain or conflict to transform.

2. When you find yourself in a situation where you feel strongly about a position and are looking to make another person wrong for theirs, try breathing your selected quality through your heart. See what happens.

3. Express gratitude more often – to your partner, family, friends, and colleagues. It might not feel comfortable initially, but it will become more natural with time.

Additional Resources

Barasch, Marc Ian. *Field Notes on the Compassionate Life: A Search for the Soul of Kindness*. Rodale Inc., 2005.

Institute of Noetic Sciences: www.noetic.org

Pearce, Joseph Chilton, *The Biology of Transcendence*. Rochester VT. Park Street Press, 2002.

5. BRIDGING AND INQUIRY

Compassionate Listening is adaptable to any conflict. The listening requires a particular attitude – non-judgmental, non-adversarial, and seeks the truth of the person questioned. It also seeks to see through any masks of hostility and fear to the sacredness of the individual.

-Gene Knudsen Hoffman

Many of us have experienced the frustration of beginning to share a concern or problem with someone and having that person ask or say something that steers the conversation in a totally different direction. We may end up either feeling let down or resentful that yet another opportunity to just be heard was lost.

Among the skills of being a Compassionate Listener is knowing when and how to ask questions that lead the speaker into a deeper inquiry about an unresolved issue or conflict. Asking questions that do this is an art form that originates with the heart's intention.

Questions can interrupt the flow of a speaker's story, so make sure to use your questions sparingly and with clarity about your purpose. And although we don't usually know how our questions will affect another person, with keen observation and listening with all of our senses, we'll soon find out.

Skilled inquiry can encourage people to delve more deeply into their own internal suitcase as they seek to unpack its contents. Or it can lead people out of the heart and into a heady analysis – or perhaps into a place of tighter constriction and self-protection. The best way to breathe life into the exploration is to ask open-ended questions that promote movement beyond a place of stuckness.

As a Compassionate Listener, it is critical to hold respect (and not judgment) for where the speaker currently is. The challenge is to offer an opening that might be just what the speaker needs in order to inch into new territory and gain deeper understanding.

Skilled compassionate inquiry rarely begins with the word "why," which all too often can make someone feel a need to justify an emotion, perspective or behavior. That, in turn, can have the opposite effect of the one you want: it may close, rather than open, the door to a deeper understanding. Consider asking questions that begin with gentle words like, "I'm wondering...," or "I'm curious about..."

THE ART OF THE QUESTION

So what's the measure of a skillful question? Primarily, it's anything that provides a portal for the speaker to explore new territory beyond the potentially stuck places of an often-repeated story.

As in the Quaker tradition of a Clearness Committee, Compassionate Listeners use inquiry in a healing way with the intent of helping the speaker delve more deeply, rather than as a means to satisfy the listener's curiosity. That's an important distinction.

Take your cue from the speaker. By carefully observing his or her verbal and nonverbal response, you'll know how you're doing; that is, whether you're being of service or not.

Use questions sparingly, knowing that:

- Questions can interrupt the flow.
- Silence may be the greatest gift you can offer.
- When you ask a question with the intention of criticizing, showing off your knowledge or fixing the situation, you are not being a Compassionate Listener in that moment.

Examples of questions that can serve:

- Could you say more about that?
- Can you help me understand?
- What was it like for you?
- How has the situation affected your life?

- Where do you find hope in this situation?
- Disputes often reach the levels they do because of deep, unmet needs. Do you sense any unmet needs in this situation?
- If this situation were fully resolved, how would things be better for you?
- If you were a wise fly on the wall viewing this issue, what do you think might work?
- What's the source of your courage?
- What life experiences have helped you in this situation?
- What's your highest vision for what this situation might look like if you're able to move beyond where it is?

Self-Inquiry

Being able to offer the gift of listening to another person is a key piece of our practice. Yet, it's something so many of us fail to bring to ourselves. And, like everything else, it's a practice to cultivate.

So this next exercise is about listening – to you. It's a journaling exercise that will help you explore a confusing or troubling situation in your own life for the sake of gaining a deeper understanding into its personal meaning.

- Write a brief summary of the situation.
- Ask yourself some deepening questions that might enhance your understanding of it. Check the options listed earlier in this chapter for ideas of what some deepening questions might be that could serve your exploration.
- If there's a question you've been avoiding asking yourself that might shed light on *your* role in this situation, ask it now.
- Answer the questions you've chosen to explore.

This exercise is just for you, so don't censor what you write! Remember that the heart carries a great deal of wisdom, and inquiry that elicits a response from the head rarely holds the same potential for insight and healing as inquiry that promotes exploration of the heart. After completing the exercise, review what you've written and see if you've learned anything new.

BRIDGING TO CONNECT WITH ANOTHER PERSON

Learning how to connect in a way that opens another person to further, positive interaction with you is helpful in many situations. And it is an important Compassionate Listening skill to cultivate.

Sometimes when faced with a difficult person – perhaps someone we disagree with or find unreasonable – we decide that trying to talk with them is a losing battle that is not worth the effort. In doing this, we exclude the person from the tribe of the worthy, which can be a disservice to them as well as to us. It may also be a sign of our own arrogance.

Compassionate Listening offers us a choice, so that when we do choose to remain in relationship with another person, we're able to bring greater intention and skill to our efforts.

There are other times when we would like to be in contact with another person, but find that something we say turns them off to us. How can we attune ourselves to the smallest indications that this is happening and try out another, more effective attempt?

In both of these situations, bringing the skill of Bridging to Connect can be important in transforming the energy of conflict or disengagement into an opportunity for further understanding and deeper connection.

> *If you can see me and hear me, and I can see you and hear you, this is one of the starting points. We need to allow ourselves to truly see each other..."*
>
> *- Farhan*
> *Former Mayor, HAMAS Party, West Bank*

The goal of the next exercise is to become more intentional and skilled at making authentic heart-to-heart connection with another. It is divided into two parts: reflective listening and the more advanced skill of inquiry. We separate the two in order to help the practitioner experience the distinctive difference between these skills.

Part One: Bridging to Connect using Reflective Listening

Step-By-Step Guidelines:

1. Ask your partner to share something with you about a current conflict. It could be about a relationship with a family member, a colleague, or perhaps a confusing situation. The only requirement is for the person sharing to choose a personal situation into which s/he would like to gain more insight. (Limit this to three to five minutes.)

2. Take a moment to ask yourself what type of reflection the person may need most in order to feel heard. Craft reflections using the skills you learned in the *Facts/Feelings/Values* exercise that will encourage your partner to want to further his or her own exploration into what's at the heart of the matter.

3. Try out the *bridging reflections* you've come up with. Your job is to intuit what might be of greatest service to the person. Your only goal at this point is for your partner's heart to be or remain open.

If your partner finds your reflections to be helpful, s/he'll be inclined to sink into a deeper heart-centered state. You'll know if it was useful – either by listening carefully to the person's response or by picking up body language cues. Sometimes an immediate smile, sigh of relief, or even tears can tell you that this may have been an opening to greater awareness.

Remember that a bridge coming from the heart carries different energy than a bridge coming from the head. So often it's not the specific words you use, but where they're coming from *within you* (*head* versus *heart*) that matters most.

When providing the reflection, remember to stay clear of your own analysis, interpretation, or attempt to fix the problem. And always be respectful.

Be aware that in real life, silence or a simple reflection may be the greatest gift you can offer to encourage another person to continue his/her exploration of meaning.

Part Two: Bridging to Connect using Inquiry

Step-By-Step Guidelines:

1. The speaker shares the highlights of a personal situation, or continues with the original issue shared in Part One, above.

2. You, the listener, then take a moment to reflect on what the speaker shared and see if there's a question you might ask that could help your practice partner delve more deeply into his or her own understanding or experience of the situation.

3. Instead of answering the question, the speaker takes a minute to reflect on your question before giving you feedback.

4. The speaker then lets you know if your attempt was:

   • Opening – the speaker's heart stayed engaged and s/he wanted to explore further.

   • Closing – the speaker did not want to respond or was inclined to make a more intellectual response.

   • Neutral

If your question leads your partner out of the heart, explore the following reasons:

- Was there an agenda implied in your question?
- Did your attempt to connect not feel heart-based and genuine?
- Did you tend to go on and on? (We generally find that less is more.)
- Was your response more about you and how you were impacted than about the speaker?

If your question was opening, ask your partner why it worked. If it didn't work, ask your partner why it might have missed the mark. Then re-connect with your heart and try again. This is a learning opportunity for both of you.

TAKE-AWAY SUGGESTIONS

1. Practice inquiry in situations where you might otherwise be tempted to go into "fix it" mode. See what new perspective might be lurking just beneath the surface of another person's perhaps often-repeated story.

2. As a Compassionate Listening practitioner, ask yourself what your intention is in asking questions. Is it to satisfy your own curiosity, make a point, or urge a specific action? Or is it truly to be of service in helping the other person explore new or deeper terrain? If it's the latter, and with their permission, move forward!

Additional Resources

Palmer, Parker. *A Hidden Wholeness: The Journey Toward an Undivided Life*. Jossey-Bass, C. 2009.

Peavey, Fran. *Strategic Questioning: An Experiment in Communication of the Second Kind*. Available from crabgrass@igc.org.

6. CONFLICT AS OPPORTUNITY

You never know what a teabag is like until it's in hot water.

-Unknown

Many of us grew up thinking that conflict was bad and something to avoid at all costs. Yet for others of us, conflict was a normal part of our family or community culture, and perhaps even something that was expected and rewarded. Some of us will do almost anything to steer clear of conflict, while others seem to enjoy the drama and stimulation of an adversarial situation or a good argument. The sport of debate is threaded throughout our school systems, political structures and in many families as well. It's all too often a game with winners and losers.

Since we are each unique beings, with different needs and experiences, conflict is inevitable. It's not bad – it just is. So how do we make conflict serve us in the very best way it can – as an opportunity to bring greater understanding and healing to our world? If it sounds like a strange contradiction...read on!

THE VALUE OF CONFLICT

In the heat of conflict, the question of our intention becomes paramount. And we have a choice. We can use conflict as an opportunity to learn about ourselves and grow...or not. We can choose to stay in relationship with the other person...or not. If we choose to stay in connection, what's our motivation? Is it truly to understand ourselves and our conflict partner better? Or is to change the other person, find the flaw in his or her thinking or make the other person wrong?

Ask yourself if you're ready to take on the courageous work of becoming a peacemaker in your daily life – or at least in some situations. And be honest. Refrain from judging yourself harshly if you're not quite ready. Another time may be just the right time!

Learning through conflict is a journey that can ultimately lead to less fear, greater self-knowledge, and deeper intimacy with others. Yet, much like the journey of a mountain climber, the process can be a rocky road with much uncertainty along the way. You'll need to be committed, have the right equipment (in this case, a toolkit of skills), and be willing to align with others who can support you in staying healthy and connected to your deepest essence.

But first, it helps not to be wedded to the outcome. The process of managing conflict well – and with integrity – holds many gifts for you, no matter what ends up happening between you and the other person. As with climbing, however, you must listen to the cues that tell you when conditions have become too treacherous and you may need to wait or turn back. In the case of conflict, always protect yourself from physical harm.

When you're faced with a specific conflict, ask yourself the following question: Is this the right person, the right place and the right time to step deeper into the experience? If the answer is yes, this chapter will give you some of the tools you'll need to make sense of and manage what arises.

EXPLORING YOUR RELATIONSHIP TO CONFLICT

The following exercises can help prepare you for unpacking conflicts and harvesting their gifts. They can be done either alone, with a practice partner, or in a practice group.

Your Attitude Toward Conflict

Ask yourself the following questions and answer honestly:

- How comfortable are you with conflict?
- Do you have a lot of conflict in your life?
- How was conflict role-modeled in your family?
- What did you learn at school about dealing with conflict?
- How well do you navigate conflict?

Be a Fair Witness to your challenges with conflict. Read what you've written, suspending self-judgment and bringing compassion to yourself for whatever may have caused discomfort with managing the conflicts in your life. If you're doing this exercise with other people, share your insights and reflections with them.

WHOSE TRUTH IS RIGHT?

Establishing the truth is a tricky business. That's because vastly different viewpoints can exist about what the facts of a situation really are and who bears the greatest responsibility for the problem. Yet, establishing whose version of reality is correct is the basis of most conflicts, both large and small – in families, communities, between political parties, and among nations. These kinds of debates often lead to despair, rather than enlightenment.

This complicated interplay of narratives is what can make a conflict so interesting to explore, yet so challenging to resolve. People can spend a lifetime looking at the past, struggling to determine who was to blame for a previous hurt, and then not forgiving the person they believe perpetrated the wrong. Locked in place, the unhealed pain is passed on to others and often unwittingly transmitted from one generation to the next. All around us we witness long-standing repercussions of family violence, tribal feuds, and wars among nations wreaking havoc on today's innocent victims.

It's imperative in these turbulent times to be able to loosen the grip on our own version of reality enough to see that other versions of truth exist.

Imagine two people looking through opposite windows into the same house. Each sees a different view, and neither sees the whole. Whose view is real? The obvious answer is "both." Only when you are able to get to the other person's window, step into his or her shoes and look at what s/he sees will you

know that his or her perspective is also real. The more windows there are, the more versions of reality there are likely to be.

We view situations through many lenses – both individual and cultural. Some of the cultural influences include gender, age, culture, religion, and socio-economic class. Recognizing all of the perspectives at play, it is no wonder that we experience things so differently.

The *impact* a statement has on the listener may not at all be what the speaker intended. Yet we often frame our responses as if someone else were responsible for how we feel. For example, we say things like "you make me angry" or "you hurt me" rather than acknowledging that it is our interpretation about what was said or done that causes the feelings. Our work as Compassionate Listeners is to unpack the story, separating impact from intention, and share our feelings and perspectives without judgment or blame.

WHAT TRIGGERS YOU?

Each of us has different cues that let us know we're treading in troubled and triggering waters. For some people, the signs are obvious physiological ones, like a speedy heartbeat, flushed face, bodily shaking or an off feeling in the gut. Telltale signs for others could be a rapid onset of confusion, coupled by an inability to speak with any semblance of clarity or to make even the simplest of decisions.

Our immediate reactions are often designed to protect us. The *fight-flight-or-freeze* response is an instinct of the *reptilian* brain that lives within all of us. Unmitigated, it prompts us into one of several familiar behaviors that most of us know all too well: to defend, blame, retaliate, or totally withdraw. All of these reactions can result in fueling the fire of conflict and deepening the chasm between us and the other person.

Fortunately, a more sophisticated brain resides within each of us as well – one that moves us beyond protective instinct toward reasoned thought and the capacity to make wise choices. To access this part of our brain requires both the desire and the tools to manage our triggers and act more skillfully.

Tips for managing triggers:

1. Recognize you're triggered. Learn to recognize your earliest warning signs.
2. Take a pause. Stop, Center, and Breathe. Breathing deeply and slowly is often the quickest way to regain equanimity and release a trigger. You might also try breathing compassion in and through your heart.
3. Become curious. Ask yourself:
   - What old hurts might this conflict be tapping into?
   - How do my judgments about myself and the other person contribute to the conflict?
   - What values do I hold dear that weren't respected in this situation?
   - What do I want or need in order to feel seen and heard in this situation?
4. Act wisely. Remember and use the Five Core Practices referred to in Chapter 2.

Recognizing Triggers

How do you know when you're triggered? Use the Trigger Recognition Worksheet to help you identify the first signs of your triggered state – on a physical, emotional, mental and spiritual level.

When triggered, people often lose access to their heart and its deeper wisdom. A key skill for the Core Practice of Developing the Fair Witness is to notice at the earliest possible moment when you're triggered. Take some time to think about the signs, symptoms, and sensations you experience.

TRIGGER RECOGNITION WORKSHEET

Body Physical sensations & actions	Mind Thoughts	Emotions Feelings	Spirit Sense of connection
My heart beats rapidly	I get totally inarticulate	I get angry	I feel isolated and all alone in the world
My face gets flushed		I feel panicky	

Self-Calming

Create a list of what you can and may already do to calm yourself and find your center, once triggered. List actions for both in the moment and after the fact. It might help to share your list with friends and find out how they re-center when triggered. There's a wealth of techniques to draw from, and you never know when you'll come across ones that might work for you.

The categories in the Self-Calming Worksheet may be useful to you. And remember, this is for you, so don't worry if you can't figure out which category something belongs in. The idea is simply to bring options that work for you into conscious awareness.

SELF-CALMING WORKSHEET

Body	Mind	Emotions	Spirit
I focus on breathing through my heart	I imagine the other person as a young child	I express compassion for myself	I take a walk in nature
I touch my hand to my heart	I think of things I appreciate about the other person	I make myself a cup of soothing tea	I listen to classical music

Freeze Frame: Transforming Stress and Conflict

This meditation is based on the work of Doc Lew Childre, Institute of HeartMath. Take your time with it. In fact, you may wish to have a friend walk you through it or you may wish to audiotape the directions, with appropriate spaces, letting your own voice lead you through it.

Bring to mind a stressful situation or conflict you've been hooked into...one you'd like to find a new way to deal with. Feel the stress this situation evokes in your body as you put yourself fully into that situation. Notice your thoughts... your feelings...

Now "Freeze the Frame" and choose to set aside these thoughts and feelings... Bring your attention to your breath and shift your focus to the area around your heart. Imagine you're breathing through your heart to help focus your energy there. Keep your focus there for 10 seconds or more.

Call to mind a moment of deep joy or gratitude – perhaps a favorite spot in nature or an experience with another special person in your life ... Put yourself fully into this moment and re-experience it with the same feelings of warmth and deep appreciation. Feel the joy in your heart...spreading throughout your body with each breath...

*And now, **ask** your heart what would be a wise response to the conflict situation – one that will minimize future stress. Listen to what your heart says in answer to your question.*

Trigger Response Plan

This is an opportunity to develop a plan for managing a situation that you know typically triggers you into a reactive state. Write down a brief description of the situation. When does it occur and with whom? How do you know when you're triggered? What can you do to re-center yourself into a clear-thinking, non-reactive state?

The journal entries below give an example of how this might work:

I am typically triggered when I begin talking to my sister-in-law Veronica about an issue that concerns me, and she immediately switches the focus of attention to herself and her own problems.

I know that I'm triggered when I start feeling really angry and begin to withdraw, thinking that this woman just doesn't have a clue about how to listen.

I can calm myself down by putting my hand on my heart and remembering what a devoted wife Veronica is to my brother and how much that means to me. I can also have compassion for both myself and for Veronica.

What I really want is for Veronica just to listen to me and perhaps ask deepening questions. Maybe we can even practice that together!

(Optional) What I'm willing to do about that is talk to Veronica and explain to her what my concern is and what I would like to happen the next time I talk to her about a problem I'm having.

It may be that just having this awareness is your first step. If you decide not to talk to Veronica, that's OK, too. If you talk to Veronica, remember to use "I" statements rather than language of blame. When you speak from your heart, it is likely to reach and open the heart of the other person.

TAKE-AWAY SUGGESTIONS

1. Keep a trigger journal for a week or two. Include even the small triggers you might otherwise ignore – perhaps made noticeable by a sigh, rolling your eyes, or drumming your fingers. Review your entries in search of any patterns regarding the kinds of situations, places, people, or even the time of day when you're most triggered.

Here are some questions you might ask yourself:

- What are your earliest warning signs and behaviors?
- What other factors are present when you get triggered? Are you feeling tired, hungry, or rushed?
- Is a story about the other person or situation circling in your mind?

2. If you become triggered, try one of the practices you've identified to help you return to a more centered place. Remember not to initiate "speaking from the heart" when you're in a triggered state!

3. If you feel courageous, try talking to the person you've referred to in the *Trigger Response Plan* about your concern and what you'd like to be different. Part of showing up fully and authentically is being honest about what you want and speaking it from the heart. If the person is your friend, it's possible to ask for the kind of listening you would like in a given situation. If we never let the other person know what we want, it is likely that we'll never get it.

Additional Resources

Childre, Doc Lew and Howard Martin. *The HeartMath Solution: The Institute of HeartMath's Revolutionary Program for Engaging the Power of the Heart's Intelligence.* HarperOne, 2000.

Crum, Thomas F. *The Magic of Conflict*, 2nd edition. NY: Touchstone, 1998.

The Institute for Heartmath at www.heartmath.org

7. JUDGMENT AND BLAME: TAKING RESPONSIBILITY

Peace comes through the hard work of meeting the "other" – the human being behind the stereotype.

– The 14th Dalai Lama

As we all know, it's easy to get triggered into conflict with another person. Perhaps we disagree about an issue, or we've been hurt by the other person in the past and are waiting for the next shoe to drop, or we're certain that the other person's tone of voice couches criticism or disrespect. Or maybe they've innocently used a word or phrase that lands us in a sinkhole of difficult feelings because of a past experience or painful association.

These are among the many minefields to which we may have become sensitized over the years. When someone trips over one of them, we may shut down, almost like a sea anemone that instinctively contracts to protect itself. Or we may immediately launch into a mode of attack or blame. When we go into a place of protection, other defense mechanisms may come into play as well, including judgment.

THE ROLE OF JUDGMENT

Often when we're triggered, we go into judgment of another person. Why? Because either consciously or unconsciously we decide that it may be a safer place to rest than in the vulnerability required to look at our own role in the situation. The downside of this is that in the process of judging, we lose access to the wisdom of our hearts.

Judgment isn't always a bad thing though. In fact, judgment in the best sense is about discernment – a critical skill that helps us make good decisions and wise choices. But when we become judgmental as a way of protecting ourselves, it creates a chasm between us and another person. That is counter to our intention of connection, which is at the core of being a Compassionate Listener.

Accessing our Fair Witness, we'll use the next few exercises to explore our own judgments.

Judging Ourselves

1. Make a list of the judgments you commonly tell yourself: "I never do it right; I'm not _____ enough; I'm too _____ (fill in the blank)." Some of us are more critical of ourselves than we are of others. Noticing these judgments is the first step toward breaking this often self-destructive habit.

2. Look at your list and identify your strongest negative voices with an asterisk. Seek the longing, gift or value beneath each of the judgments you've marked. Perhaps someone harshly criticizes herself for being disorganized. She might then recognize what she values in the following way: "I hate my disorganization and find my office disgusting and overwhelming. I want to use my time wisely to better serve my clients – and also to reduce my stress."

3. Bring compassion to yourself for sustaining these judgments and repeating the stories that hold them in place.

Recognizing and befriending our own critical self-judgments is important work. Sometimes we try to expel these inner voices, perhaps even violently attempting to push them away. However, making peace with them and finding out how they're trying to serve us in a positive way is our job. If we can do that with ourselves, we're more likely to be able to manage our judgment of others with equal skill and generosity.

Judging Others

Identify a person you have recently had a hard time with and look at the issue of judgments in the context of that relationship. It's helpful if this is a personal situation that still troubles you – or, even better, one that frequently repeats itself. For maximum benefit, make it something you'd like to gain more insight about.

For example, many people have sensitivities that arise repeatedly with the same person – perhaps a sibling, spouse, friend, or co-worker. Using one of these relationships would be useful in this exercise.

Step-by-Step Guidelines:

1. Who is the person you are judging? Choose a personal relationship – a friend, partner, parent, sibling, colleague, or someone else you know and not a political figure.

2. What's the situation that gives rise to your triggers? My friend Joan is very smart and opinionated. She totally dominates almost every conversation – whether it's with me alone or when there's a room full of people. There's no space for me (or anyone else for that matter) to get a word in edge-wise when she's present. We met for coffee yesterday and Joan talked nonstop the whole time. I didn't get to say anything. When this happened, I withdrew, once again, and felt angry and judgmental of her.

3. Think about your judgments of this person when his or her behavior triggers you. Be completely honest – and give yourself the time you need to identify at least three to five judgments if you can. No one else needs to see this information unless you choose to share it.

4. Now think about what values you hold dear that are violated in this situation.

5. The last step is to think about what values the other person (Joan in this case) might hold that motivate the behavior you're judging. Just guess at this. Most often, you'll be pretty accurate. But even if you're not right – just the process of stepping outside of the situation and trying to inhabit the other person's world can be helpful.

JUDGMENT WORKSHEET

Your Judgment	Your Values	Her/His Values (your best guess)
Joan's totally self-centered	Being valued	Wanting to be seen and heard
Joan takes up too much space	Spaciousness and connecting with others	Wanting to be honored for her intellect
Joan's controlling	Being respected Independence	Passion & concern for the world's problems

Think back to the metaphor of the house described in Chapter Six. Depending upon whose window you were seeing through, the room would look different. This exercise provides you with one more technique to help you see through another person's lens. When you're focused only on your judgments of the other, it's likely that you'll be stuck using language that blames or maligns. However, another more skillful option is to speak from the heart about the values you hold that were violated, most likely unintentionally, in this interaction.

TAKING RESPONSIBILITY FOR YOUR ROLE

One game to play is to see if you can follow your judgment of others back to yourself. Often, when we negatively judge another person, the judgment of the other masks a quality in ourselves that we don't feel good about. If we could address that issue, our judgment of the other person would be likely to either dissolve or become irrelevant.

For example, I might complain about someone else talking all the time and taking up too much space when what I really need to focus my attention on is me: on staying present (rather than withdrawing) and having the courage to value what I have to say enough to speak it unapologetically, compassionately, and with clarity. That is *my* challenge and requires no behavioral change on the part of the other person.

If I focus more attention on what the other person should do differently than on what my role is and how to cultivate the best in *me*, then I'm on the wrong track. I'm the only person I can change!

If we look honestly at our own self-judgments, we may see some similarities between our negative *self*-judgments and the judgments we have of others. For example, I may judge another person as being selfish when I'm struggling with challenges around my own generosity and stingy heart.

Widening Circles: Stepping into the Shoes of Another

This exercise, adapted from Joanna Macy's *Widening Circles,* can be a powerful tool for cultivating compassion for yourself and others.

Widening Circles can be done as a speaking exercise with a partner or as an individual journaling exercise. I find that actually hearing my own words, in addition to writing them, provides a powerful self-listening opportunity. So even if you're journaling, you might try to speak the words out loud.

Step-by-Step Guidelines

1. Identify a challenging situation with another person that's currently unresolved. Make sure this is a conflict you would like more insight into and have a stake in resolving.

What's the personal situation you'd like to explore? Include the person and highlight the details that are most important without getting lost in the language of blame. That's important because we often repeat our stories in a way that can keep us stuck in our perspective, rather than getting to the crux of what the problem is.

When telling your story, make sure to reveal:

- What happened – be brief.
- Your feelings about what happened.
- What you most longed for that you didn't get in this situation.

If you do this in a dyad, ask your partner to coach you, if necessary, to make sure that you speak in the first person about what "I want," clearly identify your feelings, and plainly state what you want in this situation that you're not getting.

Example:

I started talking to my friend Joan about an argument I had just had with my brother. Within a few minutes, she totally commandeered the conversation and began talking all about her problems with her sister. No matter what I did to refocus on what had happened between my brother and me, she brought the issue back to herself and her situation with her sister. And this wasn't the first time this happened. I finally just shut up and stopped trying to talk about what was going on with me.

I felt so frustrated and angry – and I got really upset with her and told her she didn't know what it was like to be a good friend. Actually, I was really hurt.

What I most wanted was for her just to listen to me and give me the time I needed rather than start talking about herself and her situation. I really care about her, and I feel sad when this happens.

2. This is the challenging piece. Now step into the other person's shoes and go through the identical process you did in Step 1. But this time, tell the story from the other person's perspective and speak or write using the first person, "I."

Remember that before you step into the shoes of another person, you must first take off your own. That requires both intention and courage. Then trust that when you actually step into the other's shoes in this exercise, you're likely to find out that you know more than you think you do about your conflict partner's perspective.

Don't let the uncertainty about getting it right keep you from doing this exercise. The point is to flex your taking-off-your-shoes muscles for the sake of cultivating compassion.

Example:

My name is Joan. What happened was that (your name) got hot under the collar when I started sharing my own story about my sister. It was hurtful that she got upset so quickly. I just wanted to make her feel better and let her know that she isn't alone. But boy did she ever let me have it. Doesn't she know I care about her?

3. Take the time you need to reflect on what this exercise has been like for you. What have you learned about yourself? What have you learned about the other person?

Did this exercise alter the way you perceived the issue? If so, how? Is there a gift for you in this situation? If so, what is it?

If you're doing this exercise with another person, make sure your partner has equal time to explore his or her own story and inhabit the shoes of his/her conflict partner.

TAKE-AWAY SUGGESTIONS

1. When you become aware that you're holding a negative judgment about yourself or another person, try one or more of the exercises in this chapter to help you go deeper into your own journey of self-discovery.

2. In conflict situations, we often project our judgments and stories onto other people unless we're able to look objectively at what is happening between us, own our role in the conflict, and speak honestly and from the heart about what has gone on. This is the cleansing process needed to spur new growth and intimacy in our relationships.

Additional Resources

Macy, Joanna with Brown, Molly. *Coming Back to Life: Practices to Reconnect Our Lives, Our World.* Gabriola Island, BC, Canada: New Society Publishers, 2016.

8. THE DRAMA TRIANGLE

I can't thank you enough for the incredible gifts from last weekend. I began the week with repairing conflicts in my life…They were things I thought I had to live with and now I have moved enough to bring my peace to the situations. Thank You, Thank you.

- Participant, Compassionate Listening Introductory Training

The Drama Triangle is a dysfunctional social interaction model developed by Dr. Stephen Karpman, a Transactional Analysis practitioner. Sometimes referred to as the Rescue Triangle, it illustrates some of the traps we can fall into in a difficult interaction. In this model, there are three roles: Rescuer, Persecutor and Victim. When people are in the triangle, the roles they play may change – sometimes almost imperceptibly. This may happen many times in the course of a single interchange. Often referred to as a game, there may be many people playing in it at the same time. All of us can easily fall into the triangle at one point or another – and into one role or another, pulling others into it with us.

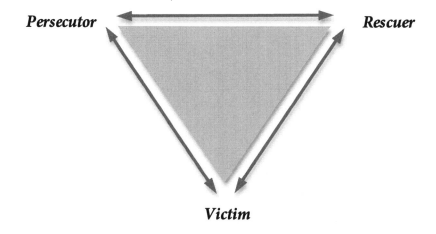

For those of us who see ourselves as caring and compassionate people, attempting to resolve another person's conflict or dilemma can be a powerful draw into the Rescuer role. Our hearts open to another person's suffering – and in the blink of an eye we take the reigns and propose strategies for what the person can or should do. Or we feel so uncomfortable with the person's suffering that we go into rescue mode for the sake of our own comfort.

Another way the urge to rescue plays out is when we witness an offense against another person and feel called to correct the injustice. We may do this by placing blame on a third party or colluding with the victim to demonize someone. In both of these cases we risk entering into a very messy situation.

As soon as we fall into the triangle in any one of the roles, we evoke one of the other roles and create a strong pull to bring someone else into the triangle with us. For example, victims need a persecutor; being seen as a persecutor means there is a victim; and rescuers do not see the victim as a self-empowered individual.

The following examples illustrate the subtle role switches that occur when the Drama Triangle is in play. After reading each of the examples, see if you can recognize at what point the players change roles. Try to think not only about the words used, but about the tone of voice and body cues, as well. Don't worry about getting it right. The purpose is just to become aware of the dynamic and how it works.

Example One

Fred and Ursula have two children. Fred's a stay-at-home dad, and Ursula's the breadwinner. This dialogue occurs after Fred has angrily disciplined his son Seth.

Ursula (trying to stay calm): *Will you just calm down? I hate it when you discipline Seth by screaming at him. He was just being a kid!*

Fred (raising his voice): *Well someone has to discipline him. You don't see what happens on a daily basis because you're never home.*

Ursula (looking down, sinking into her chair): *When you get angry, I can't talk to you.*

Fred: *Well that's your problem.*

Ursula: *It's your problem too. They're our children, you know!*

Fred (angrily): *Oh yeah, if you weren't such a workaholic, maybe you'd get more involved. (with a softer, yet sneering tone) I feel like I'm all alone in raising them...*

Ursula (impatiently): *Well why don't you just get a job? You keep saying you'll look for one, but you never do!*

Example Two

Sally and Elaine have been friends for many years and are almost like sisters. Sally has a number of physical problems and complains a lot.

Sally (almost despairing): *I'm just so upset – either it's my back pain or my stomach problems. There's always something, and I just can't stand it. I don't know what I've done to deserve this.*

Elaine (with concern): *You know, I've had back problems too. Have you thought about seeing a chiropractor?*

Sally (impatiently): *I know what's best for me. You're lucky. Your back's never been as bad as mine. And it's not only my back...*

Elaine (impatiently): *Well complaining doesn't help anything.*

Sally: *You don't understand.*

Elaine (calmly): *Well I think your attitude has a lot to do with your problems.*

Sally (angrily): *That's totally untrue. You've never understood what it's like to live in my body.*

Elaine (withdraws into silence)

In the context of our work as Compassionate Listeners, each role undermines at least one Core Practice. For example:

- A rescuer may view a victim as helpless and unable to find his/her own solution to the conflict, or may be draining him/herself to engage in a rescue operation-thus fueling both people's anger or resentment. (Core Practice undermined: Respecting Self and Others.)
- A persecutor may use verbal attack to blame another person, rather than using words or actions that have a healing intention. (Core Practice undermined: Speaking from the Heart.)
- A victim may feel helpless and angry. S/he may deny personal responsibility for how a situation has unfolded or fail to speak his or her truth without being defensive. (Core Practices undermined: Respecting Self and Others and Speaking from the Heart.)

When we find ourselves playing a role in the triangle, engaging Compassionate Listening practices can help extricate us from this destructive drama. So how can we become aware of what's happening and transform our actions into healthier behavior?

1. Listen to yourself – your body, feelings and thoughts. Is something in the interaction not feeling quite right? Are you triggered? If so, take the time to stop, center, and reflect. What are you feeling and thinking? Are you judging yourself or the other person?
2. From the place of the Fair Witness, ask yourself if you're playing a role in the triangle and, if so, which role that might be.

3. If you're in the triangle, mentally scan the Five
    Core Practices. Are there tools you've learned that might
    help you transform your actions into more skillful
    behavior? For example:

    - Refrain from blaming.

    - See yourself and the other(s) as whole and complete,
      seeking the deeper essence beneath any unskillful words
      or actions.

    - Speak your truth from the heart, using healing rather
      than hurtful language.

    - Take responsibility for your role in the conflict.

    - Recognize each person's capacity to resolve his or her
      own problem or dilemma.

    - Use reflective listening.

    - Ask a deepening question.

    - Suspend judgment.

The Five Core Practices can be your lifeline back into being a skillful Compassionate Listener.

After stepping out of the triangle, you're free to choose another path of involvement (or non-involvement) that promotes greater health. Whatever behavior you choose, however, do it with awareness and intention.

TAKE-AWAY SUGGESTIONS

1. If you've entered into the drama triangle, unpack the
    situation from the place of the Fair Witness. Which
    role(s) did you play? Which core practices might
    have helped you in this situation? What might you do
    differently in the future?

9. PRODUCTIVE DIALOGUE

The fundamental difference between creating and problem solving is simple. In problem solving we seek to make something we do not like go away. In creating, we seek to make what we truly care about exist.

– Peter Senge

One of the biggest challenges we face is how to manage our own impatience for quick resolution when hostility, anger and other indicators of conflict arise. Yet, often what's most needed in the heat of the moment is the ability to listen deeply and create the spaciousness for opening of hearts, softening of positions, and co-creation of wise action.

Compassionate Listening lays the groundwork for dialogue. Without it, a conversation can quickly devolve into debate and increasing polarity. These polarities can be as immovable as the bricks referred to in an earlier chapter, leaving little opening for the breath of new life. And without this life-giving oxygen, creative new solutions are unlikely to emerge.

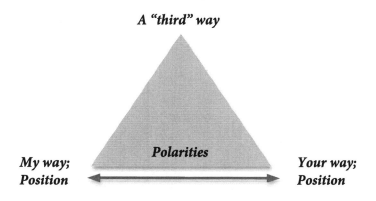

Finding a new way can be considered a spiritual challenge – one that takes us beyond the normal limitations of our minds and into unexplored territory. To get there requires engaging our hearts in the process.

In looking at the Polarities image, I'm reminded of the ancient Egyptian pyramids, at the top of which was often a temple – a place for prayer. Perhaps the challenge of finding the third way, or unimagined solution, requires an act of equal faith. One that allows us to suspend a need to know for the moment and trust that wise action can and will emerge when the time is right and all parties' concerns and deepest values have truly been heard.

INDIVIDUAL RESPONSIBILITY

Much has been written about processes to use for establishing a safe environment within which respectful dialogue can occur. Some of these resources are listed at the end of this chapter.

Holding the space for respectful dialogue is very much an individual challenge as well as a process challenge. People skilled in the practices of Compassionate Listening can influence the group field in a remarkable and powerful way. (See Chapter 4, "The Heart Matters.")

> *Traditional debate methods – arguing about facts – are pretty common ways of addressing the Tibet-China issue. Compassionate Listening is a heart-based approach that looks for the humanity behind the conflict, rather than trying to figure out who is right and who is wrong.*
>
> *-Spring Cheng*
> *Tibet-China Dialogue Project*

When entering the field of public or group dialogue, it's a good idea to prepare yourself first by reviewing Compassionate Listening Core Practices and the following specific pointers:

- Seek to understand the positive values that lie beneath the surface of a person's "position."
- Humanize, rather than demonize, someone whose position differs from yours.
- Know that listening respectfully doesn't imply agreement.
- Approach dialogue with genuine curiosity, rather than with the intent of finding the flaws in another's position.
- Be willing to suspend judgment.
- Ask questions that contribute to connection rather than defensiveness or shutting down.
- Use language that's not inflammatory.
- Notice and manage your triggers so you can return to being fully present with your heart as quickly as possible.

PRACTICES FOR GROUP DIALOGUE

Many of us who have been involved with the Compassionate Listening Project over time have learned a great deal from our experiences with groups. Here are some suggestions you might find helpful depending on the purpose and size of the group.

1. Begin any meeting, no matter how large a group, with a moment of silence to bring everyone into the present and set a clear intention.

2. Consider lighting a candle as a symbol of the intention to shed light and truth into the dialogue if you feel that would serve the group.

3. Ask people for a word or phrase that reflects an intention: perhaps a quality with which they would like to show up in this meeting. The process facilitator should model this first – perhaps by speaking a quality of "patience" or "trust" or "calm" or "openness" – whatever feels authentic in the moment.

4. Use a talking object with guidelines about how to use it. This could be any object: a stone, feather, or something more mundane. Talking objects can slow dialogue down and are visual indicators of whose time it is to speak. There are at least two ways to use a talking object:

    • Leave it in the center. Then when someone wants to speak, s/he can take it – returning it to the same place when s/he has finished.

    • Pass it from one person to the next in a circle. If someone doesn't wish to speak, s/he can just give the object to the next person. This enables everyone to have a turn to speak, rather than having the more assertive or opinionated people dominate the dialogue.

5. Set guidelines and ask people to agree upon them before beginning. Some that we often use are:

    • Refrain from interrupting.

    • Respect and share time so no one monopolizes the conversation.

    • When speaking, talk about your personal feelings and experiences, using the pronoun "I" rather than assume what others ("they") may be feeling and experiencing.

    • It's OK to express strong, honest emotions.

    • Do not make personal attacks against others in the room.

    • Try to return to a centered state if you're triggered.

6. If someone is unable to manage a trigger, ask the person to share it rather than remain in a state of anger, judgment or withdrawal. Unpacking it in a group setting, particularly if it's a small group, can help build the trust needed to move beyond separation and polarity.

7. Be attentive to the group's energy. If tension becomes palpable, empower anyone present to ask for a moment of silence. This will enable everyone to slow down and bring all participants back to full presence and the

ability to access their deepest wisdom. Then you may wish to practice reflective listening with all of the parties in the room who are aggrieved or in conflict so each feels heard.

8. End with a round of gratitude, intention-setting for returning to daily life, a meditation or a blessing. The closing of a session is as important energetically as the opening of a session.

> *Everyone has a partial truth, and we must listen, discern, and acknowledge this partial truth in everyone – particularly those with whom we disagree.*
>
> *-Gene Knudsen Hoffman*

ADDITIONAL RESOURCES

Conversation Cafe, www.conversationcafe.org

Flick, Deborah, Ph.D. *From Debate to Dialogue: Using the Understanding Process to Transform our Conversations.* Boulder, CO: Orchid Publications, 1998.

Fostering Dialogue Across Divides: A Nuts and Bolts Guide from the Public Conversations Project, www.publicconversations.org

Hoffman, Gene Knudsen, Green, Leah & Monroe, Cynthia. *Compassionate Listening: An Exploratory Sourcebook About Conflict Transformation. 2001.* Download free at www.coopcomm.org

AFTERWORD

Listening creates a holy silence. When you listen generously to people, they can hear truth in themselves, often for the first time. And in the silence of listening, you can know yourself in everyone. Eventually, you may be able to hear, in everyone and beyond everyone, the unseen singing softly to itself and to you.

– Rachel Naomi Remen, MD

You've completed this book, but the journey has just begun. We hope you will continue to journal and revisit the practices and exercises many times.

If you're interested in establishing a practice group, you can find the Compassionate Listening Project Practice Group Manual as a link on our website at www.compassionatelistening.org.

Moving beyond conflict toward healing and reconciliation is critical to creating a more compassionate and peaceful world. Without finding a way to release our pain and long-held narratives of suffering, it is not clear what kind of a future we can create – either individually or collectively.

Much has been written about the challenges and opportunities of forgiveness, as well as processes that can support efforts toward reconciliation. *Practicing the Art of Compassionate Listening* does not directly address these issues. Nonetheless, Compassionate Listening practices provide very rich soil for nurturing these endeavors. Indeed, forgiveness may arise spontaneously as we soften our hearts, listen more deeply and relax the mortar holding our old stories in place.

As you move forward, bring the gifts of mutual respect, greater love and deeper compassion to yourself and the world. And appreciate yourself for embarking on this journey. It's a journey for the courageous – and one well worth taking.

APPRECIATION

I would like to acknowledge many people who have been instrumental in the development of the Compassionate Listening Project.

Gene Knudsen Hoffman, a Quaker and committed international peacemaker, pioneered Compassionate Listening as a tool for reconciliation in the 1980's. Gene considered Thich Nhat Hanh, a Buddhist monk, writer and scholar, to be one of her greatest teachers and mentors and the inspiration for her Compassionate Listening work. Gene died peacefully in July 2010 in Santa Barbara, CA. We honor her and the important lineage of this work.

Leah Green, founder of the Compassionate Listening Project, has held the vision for this work for many years, and her passion and tireless dedication have helped sustain our work through many difficult times. Her pursuit of this vision continues to have a transformative impact on the lives of many people.

Carol Hwoschinsky was the training director of the Compassionate Listening Project from 1998 to 2007. She introduced many of us to the teachings of great and inspirational thinkers in diverse fields. Carol continues to be a mentor to us all. Additionally, she is the author of *Listening With the Heart*, the first book ever written about the Compassionate Listening Project's work.

Susan Partnow is a tireless and talented Compassionate Listening facilitator and senior trainer. In addition to having served on the Compassionate Listening Board of Directors, Susan was co-creator of the Advanced Training curriculum. She is a valued partner and collaborator in this work.

Brian Berman, Karen Bonnell, Eryn Kalish and Susan Partnow served with me on the Compassionate Listening Project's Core Council. Between 2003 and 2006, together with Leah Green and Carol Hwoschinsky, the Core Council conceptualized our Five Core

Practices and worked countless hours to develop a curriculum that could bring this work more widely into our world.

Since that time, we have continued to evolve our work with the help of the many people who have participated in delegations to Israel and Palestine, in our reconciliation work with Jews and Germans, and those who have attended our workshops in this country and abroad. Thanks to each and every one of them for trusting us as guides on these journeys and for teaching us so much in the process.

In addition, I would like to thank all of the people in our learning community – both facilitators and those on the path toward becoming certified Compassionate Listening facilitators – for their commitment to our practices and their willingness to use them with integrity in navigating their own challenges.

I offer my deepest appreciation to Neva Welton, Linn DeNesti, Cathy Keene Merchant, and Avril Orloff, whose extraordinary talents were generously offered in the areas of editing, layout and design.

On a personal note, I would like to give special thanks to my husband Norman and my sister Ronna. Repeatedly sitting "in the fire" with me, they help me to practice the fine points of being a Compassionate Listener in the heat of real-life conflict. They are truly my greatest supporters and my most honored teachers.

Andrea Cohen
March 2011